CW01338533

PLEASE NOTE: ADULT SUPERVISION IS REQUIRED

Please always carefully follow any instructions given and supervise your child during any of the activities described in this book – especially those involving piercing or cutting objects.

GENERAL SAFETY ADVICE:

Always close scissors after use and put lids on glue. Be careful handling any pieces of plastic or kebab sticks that may have sharp edges, and always put away all materials safely after use. Ask an adult before using glue and before using a high-pressure bicycle pump, and wear eye protection when required.

FOR MY MUM AND DAD – FOR ALWAYS BEING THERE WHENEVER I NEEDED A PIT STOP – F.S.

First published 2023 by Walker Books Ltd, 87 Vauxhall Walk, London SE11 5HJ

2 4 6 8 10 9 7 5 3 1

Text © 2023 Fran Scott   Illustrations © 2023 Paul Boston

The right of Fran Scott and Paul Boston to be identified as author and illustrator respectively of this work has been asserted in accordance with the Copyright, Designs and Patents Act 1988

This book has been typeset in Din

Printed in China

All rights reserved. No part of this book may be reproduced, transmitted or stored in an information retrieval system in any form or by any means, graphic, electronic or mechanical, including photocopying, taping and recording, without prior written permission from the publisher.

British Library Cataloguing in Publication Data: a catalogue record for this book is available from the British Library

ISBN 978-1-4063-9025-4

www.walker.co.uk

HOW TO BUILD A
RACING CAR

 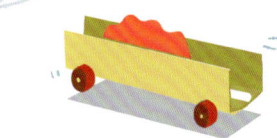   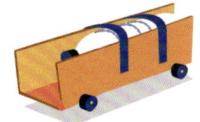

FRAN SCOTT   Illustrated by PAUL BOSTON

ABOUT ME

My name is Fran, and I'm one of those lucky people who absolutely LOVES their job.

I'm a "maker", which means I get to build all manner of interesting things. I mostly design science demonstrations: props to explain the answers to scientific questions. Questions like "Why is the sky blue?" or "How is poo made?"

I'm also a pyrotechnician – which means I can set things on fire. Not just so that the fire looks cool, but also so that everyone around me is safe (and yes, it's as brilliant as it sounds).

I've used these skills in loads of science and engineering shows: in schools, theatres and on television. I'm also a presenter, so do keep an eye out for me if you're watching CBBC or BBC Bitesize. (I won't hear you saying "Hi", but feel free to try it.)

But that's enough about me, because this book is about YOU. To be precise, it's about you making something awesome, and hopefully having fun as you go.

ABOUT BUILDING THINGS

When I was at school, I used to read a lot of books about making things – and I loved them. But I always got annoyed if the thing I was building didn't quite work, or looked … well, a bit rubbish.

As I got older, I began to realize that it's the actual process of making something that matters, rather than whatever it is you have at the end. Those moments where you get confused, think you can't do it and then somehow suddenly figure it out – *they're* the important ones. It's in these moments that your skills really start to improve.

So just remember, when you're reading this book: making things is fun, and making mistakes is part of the process – so don't worry if things go a bit wrong. (Having said that, I've thought hard about the design of this racing car, and tested it loads of times, so hopefully – hopefully! – this book will guide you in a step-by-step way that works for you.) So, it's time to discover exactly how to build a racing car…

RACING CAR

THIS IS A RACING CAR: THE KIND YOU SEE ZOOMING AROUND THE TRACK OF A FORMULA 1 (F1) RACE. IT'S MADE FROM MORE THAN 5,000 DIFFERENT PARTS — YOU CAN SEE SOME OF THE MOST IMPORTANT ONES IN THE LABELS.

YOUR CAR

A top-of-the-range F1 car can cost tens of millions of pounds, so I do hope you've saved up your pocket money... I'm joking, of course. Your car is going to be just as awesome, but made of much cheaper parts, so by the end of this book you will have a brilliant car you can race yourself. (And you'll still have all your pocket money.)

YOU WILL NEED

There are two ways of building your car – the low-tech (pages 26–29) or high-tech way (pages 30–33) – and you'll need slightly different things for each one. Look at the lists below to see which you want to try. Be canny: recycle what you can, and collect the cardboard from old delivery boxes. You'll need all the stuff from the "Every car" list, plus what's on the list for the version you're making.

EVERY CAR

- 30 cm by 17.5 cm piece of corrugated cardboard
- 4 pieces of really stiff cardboard (1 x 50 cm by 10 cm, 1 x 54 cm by 9 cm and 2 x 10 cm by 40 cm)
- Ruler (the longer, the better)
- Pencil
- Another pencil (a sharp one)
- Scissors (ideally with a pointy end)
- Wooden kebab sticks (at least 15 cm long) (x2)
- Wooden kebab sticks (at least 20 cm long – or you can stick shorter ones together) (x2)
- 12 cm by 5 cm pieces of paper (x2)
- Sticky tape
- PVC tape (sometimes called electrical tape)
- Matching bottle tops (the ones from fizzy drinks bottles are best) (x4)
- All-purpose glue
- Sticky tack (a pea-sized amount)
- 60 cm piece of string
- Sunglasses or safety goggles

LOW-TECH: BALLOON ENGINE

- Balloon (normal round shape and size)
- 4-pint plastic milk bottle (empty and clean)
- Balloon pump

HIGH-TECH: BOTTLE ENGINE

- 500 ml plastic drinks bottle with a lid (a fizzy drink bottle works well, as it's made of strong plastic)
- An inner tube from a bicycle tyre (it doesn't have to be new – ask if your local bike shop has any spare, broken ones)
- Pen
- Sharp, pointy object (like pointy scissors, corkscrew or keys)
- Bicycle pump (with a pressure gauge)
- Lighter and heatproof glove (optional)

There are some finishing touches you can add to your car – look at pages 48, 50 and 52 for what you'll need.

GET YOUR SCIENCE UP TO SPEED

Hang on, we can't have you building a car without ANY training, can we? Consider the next few pages your (crash!) course on becoming a racing car engineer.

When it comes to building a racing car – a marvellous piece of technology capable of travelling at a WHOPPING 360 km per hour – understanding the science behind how it moves is the secret to keeping the driver safe. Also, it's only by knowing the tiniest scientific details behind what you're doing that you can then find out just how far to push the boundaries and make the best racing car possible.

The science behind racing cars is all about FORCES. It's about knowing which forces slow you down, which forces make you go fast, how these forces can change at different speeds, and which forces will help you become a Jedi Master (that last one is optional, obviously).

CHECK OUT ALL THE FORCES ON THIS CAR AND YOU'LL SEE WHAT I MEAN...

DRIVING FORCE

This is the force that "drives" the car forwards. In a Formula 1 car, this force is made when the tyres push down onto the road. The more contact the tyres have with the road, the higher this force will be – and the higher this force is, the faster the car goes.

Also, the higher this force is, the more likely it is that the car will be able to go fast around corners without skidding.

LIFT

As a car drives through the air, the air moves around it and this produces several forces. One of the forces acts to lift the car off the ground – appropriately called "lift". The more lift, the slower the car goes.

WEIGHT

Yup, weight is actually a force. The more the car weighs, the higher this force is and so the more driving force you'll need to make your car go fast.

Let's think about it: which is easier to throw fast, a bowling ball or a football? The football, right? That's because it weighs less, and it's easier to make lighter things go faster (accelerate) – and everyone wants a racing car that is easy to make go fast.

DOWNFORCE

And then there's downforce, which acts (surprise, surprise) in a downwards direction towards the road.

The more downforce, the faster the car goes. That's because the downforce pushes the tyres to have more contact with the road – which gives you more driving force.

DRAG

Drag is another force which is caused by the air as the car moves through it. With drag, the air pushes the opposite way from the direction in which the car is moving – and so, this slows the car down.

DID YOU KNOW?

THE STUDY OF HOW AIR INTERACTS WITH OBJECTS AS THEY MOVE THROUGH IT IS CALLED "AERODYNAMICS". IT'S A GREEK WORD, WITH "AERO" MEANING "AIR" AND "DYNAMICS" COMING FROM "DYNAMIKÓS", MEANING "POWERFUL". IF AN OBJECT CUTS THROUGH THE AIR EASILY, IT IS SAID TO BE "AERODYNAMIC".

TO SUM UP

So you want to go fast, right? To go fast, you need: a BIG driving force and a SMALL weight. You also need a BIG downforce and a SMALL lift. Basically, those forces shown in green make you go fast, so you want them to be as big as possible. And those forces in red slow you down, so you want them to be as small as possible.

Keeping up? Good. But, hold my hammer, why is drag orange? Drag is complicated. Drag does slow you down, but if you want any downforce at all (and you want a lot to go fast), then you'll always (unfortunately) get at least a little bit of drag thrown in for free. And this means that designing a racing car is a wonderfully delicate balance between all of these forces.

That's why it takes more than one person to build a racing car. So, what are you waiting for?

LET'S MEET THE MEMBERS OF A RACING CAR TEAM!

WELCOME TO THE TEAM

IT TAKES PEOPLE WITH ALL KINDS OF SKILLS TO MAKE A RACING CAR. HERE ARE SOME OF THE PEOPLE WHO MAKE UP THE ENGINEERING TEAM...

You may have seen me in the pit stop. In my team we can change four wheels, wipe the mirrors and the driver's visor, and make small changes to the racing car in just over two seconds. And yes, that does take a lot of practice.

I come up with the plan for race days. It's my job to understand what's happening with the weather and the conditions on the track, so I can come up with the best plan for when to make pit stops and the types of tyres that should be used.

It's not like you order a racing car online and it gets delivered with instructions – we design these things from scratch, which means we need new parts all the time ... parts that just don't exist yet! That's where I come in: I build and shape the exact part that is required.

I'm part of a huge team of designers, and we each work on our own specialist area: some of us look at the materials used to make a racing car, some at the mechanical parts and others at the electronic components. Each new design, no matter how small, gets tested and analysed, with us making adjustments until the part does exactly what is needed.

My job is all to do with how air affects how fast a racing car goes. I use Computational Fluid Dynamics (CFD) to add different parts on to a computer-based version of a car. If these tests go well, I then test the new part on a real-life model of the car in a huge wind tunnel, to see if it will actually make the car go faster or not.

DESIGN ENGINEER

AERODYNAMICIST

I work with the driver to ensure that the racing car is used to its best ability during the actual races. In my team, we look at all the data coming in from the sensors on the car and, using our plan, we make decisions about the best way to react to what is happening. I'm also the only one who talks to the driver during a race, and I coach them to perform at their best.

In racing, we use a lot of computer systems for everything from drawing car designs to testing how these designs might (or might not) work. Also, the car is fitted with thousands of sensors that tell us lots of information during a race. It is my job to come up with computer systems that are not only easy to use but that also make all that information make sense.

RACE ENGINEER

TRAINING DONE!
AND LEAVING THE BEST TEAM MEMBER TILL LAST, WE, OF COURSE, HAVE YOU! SO FASTEN YOUR SEAT BELT AND LET'S HIT THE ROAD — THE ROAD TOWARDS BUILDING YOUR VERY OWN RACING CAR.

CHAPTER ONE
THE CHASSIS

YOUR HAND MAY BE THROBBING FROM ALL THE HANDSHAKING, YOUR THOUGHTS RACING AS YOU TRY TO REMEMBER EVERYONE'S NAMES AND YOUR FACE ACHING FROM ALL THE SMILING, BUT WHAT A DAY! EVERYONE: GATHER ROUND, GATHER ROUND AND MEET THE NEWEST MEMBER OF THE FORMULA 1 AMATEUR RACING TEAM (OR "F.A.R.T." AS THEY'RE KNOWN IN THE INDUSTRY) ... THAT'S YOU!

WHAT'S THAT? YOU CAN'T WAIT TO START BUILDING?
WELL, WHY DIDN'T YOU JUST SAY?

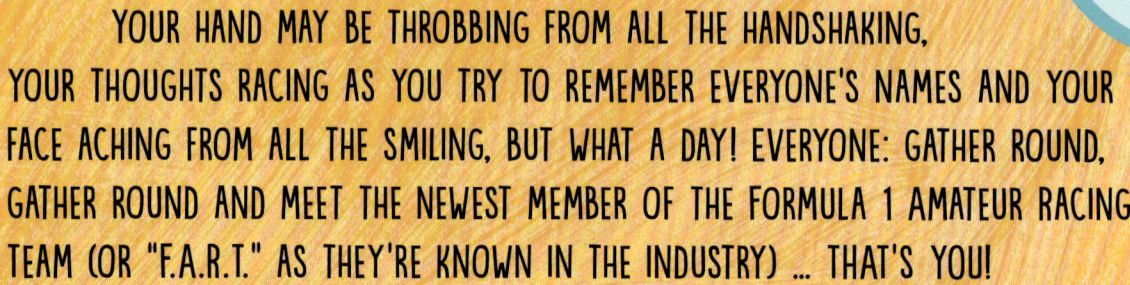

DID YOU KNOW?
WHEN A MATERIAL IS HEAVY, BENDY, SOGGY, FURRY OR GOOEY, THESE FEATURES ARE CALLED THE PROPERTIES OF THE MATERIAL. THEY'RE ALL TO DO WITH HOW A MATERIAL LOOKS AND HOW IT ACTS – AND BY THINKING ABOUT A MATERIAL'S PROPERTIES, YOU CAN WORK OUT WHICH JOBS IT WILL BE BEST FOR.

TASK ONE: BUILD THE ENTIRE CAR
Just kidding! You're going to start by focusing on the "body" of the car – so, the bit that actually makes it look car-like (just with no wheels or engine, for now).

THE BRIEF
The wheels and engine, and not forgetting the driver, all need to go somewhere – so, the car needs a body for these things to sit in or be attached to. We call the car's body the "chassis", which is pronounced "sha-see".

However, from your training task, you'll know that the heavier the car, the harder it is to make it go fast. So you need to design a chassis that is BIG enough for the necessary additions (wheel, engine and driver!), LIGHT enough to allow

the car to accelerate speedily and STRONG enough to protect the driver if there's a crash.

But you're an engineer now, and engineers laugh in the face of these kinds of roadblocks. Let's start by breaking this down into smaller problems that you can tackle one by one.

15

 ## PROBLEM ONE: THE CHASSIS NEEDS TO BE BIG AND LIGHT.

Making something big and light means you need to use a material that has a low "density". Density is literally a measure of how heavy something is compared with its size.

If a material has a LOW density it means that, even when you have a lot of it, it's still light – a good example is polystyrene packaging. Even a HUGE sheet of polystyrene is so light that it would make Mr McNo-Muscles look like an Olympic weightlifter.

Now, all of this means that your car chassis should be made of a material that has a **LOW density**.

PROBLEM TWO: THE CHASSIS NEEDS TO BE BIG AND LIGHT AND STRONG.

This means you need a material that has a low density, but which is also strong. That's not easy, as most materials that have a low density tend to also be pretty weak ... a car made out of polystyrene isn't going to get very far.

This is where "composite materials" can help. Composite materials are where two or more different materials (usually

DID YOU KNOW?

IN ORDER TO MAKE RACES FAIR AND SAFE, EACH SEASON THERE IS A MINIMUM WEIGHT A FORMULA 1 CAR IS ALLOWED TO BE. FOR 2022 THIS WAS 798 KILOGRAMS, INCLUDING THE DRIVER AND TYRES. THAT'S THE WEIGHT OF ABOUT TEN BODYBUILDERS!

with different properties) have been combined into one new material, which has all of the properties of the materials that you started with.

One example is carbon fibre (technically called carbon fibre reinforced plastic). This is made of strands of carbon (which are strong and durable) mixed with plastic (which has a low density). That means carbon fibre can make things that are **big, light AND strong** ... just perfect for a racing car chassis.

SOLUTION

It makes sense to build your chassis with a composite material – but you can't exactly pop down to your local supermarket and ask for a sheet of carbon fibre. However, you CAN ask for some corrugated cardboard, and (believe it or not) that, too, is a composite material.

We're not talking your ordinary sheet-cardboard here, but the kind that packaging boxes are made from: two sheets of cardboard with a wavy sheet sandwiched between them. Corrugated cardboard has low density and it's strong, so it's what you're going to use to make your car's chassis.

Solution found. So, what are you waiting for? Get building!

WAVY SHEET OF CARDBOARD   FLAT SHEETS OF CARDBOARD

17

MAKING THE CHASSIS

WHAT YOU'LL NEED

30 CM BY 17.5 CM PIECE OF CORRUGATED CARDBOARD

RULER (15 CM IS FINE)

PENCIL

SCISSORS (IDEALLY WITH A POINTY END)

WOODEN KEBAB STICKS (AT LEAST 15 CM LONG) (X2)

12 CM BY 5 CM PIECES OF PAPER (X2)

TAPE

MATCHING BOTTLE TOPS (X4)

ALL-PURPOSE GLUE

1 Take the piece of cardboard and at both ends mark 5 cm down and 5 cm up from each of its two long edges. Use these points to draw two lines across the length of the cardboard, then use these lines to fold the cardboard upwards and make a boat shape. This is the basic frame of your car.

2 Take one piece of paper and roll it loosely around a pencil to make a 12 cm long tube of paper. Use tape to stop it from unravelling and slide it off the pencil. Repeat with the second piece of paper.

ASK AN ADULT TO HELP

3 Using the scissors, carefully make a hole in the centre of each of the bottle tops. This hole must be big enough to fit the kebab stick through, but small enough to hold the lid in place once it is on the stick.

REMEMBER YOU NEED AN ADULT TO HELP YOU!

4 On two kebab sticks, measure from the non-pointy end and draw marks at 1 cm, 14 cm and 15 cm.

THESE WILL BECOME THE AXLES.

5 Thread one bottle top onto one kebab stick (top side first), going from the pointy end and pushing the bottle top to the furthest mark. Slide on one of the paper rolls.

Next, thread on another bottle lid – this time, bottom side first – and push on, until you can just see the 14 cm mark.

6 Get an adult to help you cut the kebab stick at the 15 cm mark.

7 Repeat steps 5 and 6 to make another set of wheels.

MAKE SURE THE WHEELS ARE SECURE ON THE KEBAB STICKS, BUT THAT THE STICKS CAN MOVE FREELY IN THE PAPER TUBES.

8 On the flat part at the bottom of the chassis, draw a line 5 cm in from one short end and label this side "FRONT". Then at the other short end, draw a line 3 cm in and label this side "BACK".

9 Apply glue to each of these lines and stick the rolled paper onto them, making sure they're super straight. Also, ensure the bottle tops do not catch on the cardboard when they turn. Leave to dry.

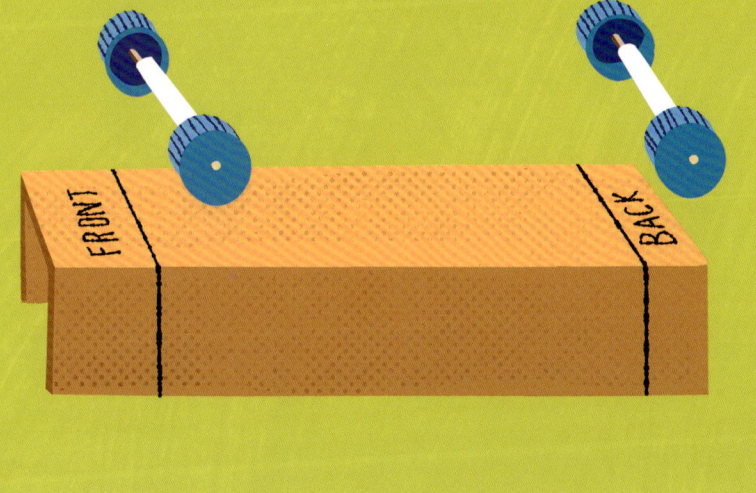

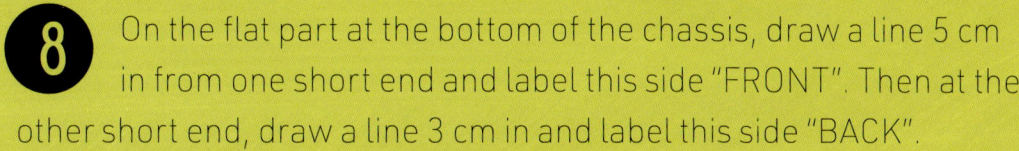

WOOHOO!

IT CAN TAKE YEARS AND YEARS TO MAKE A FORMULA 1 CAR, AND LOOK AT YOU — YOU'VE ALREADY MADE YOUR CHASSIS! YOU REALLY ARE SPEEDING AHEAD.

BUT YOU DON'T YET HAVE AN ENGINE. LUCKILY FOR YOU, THAT'S WHAT WE'LL BE SORTING OUT IN CHAPTER TWO...

CHAPTER TWO
THE ENGINE

YOU MAY NOT HAVE EVER SEEN AN ENGINE IN REAL LIFE BEFORE. WELL, MAYBE AN OLD AEROPLANE ENGINE IN A WORLD WAR II MUSEUM, BUT IT WOULDN'T HAVE FITTED ON YOUR CHASSIS ... AND I'M NOT TOO SURE HOW YOU WOULD SNEAK IT PAST THE SECURITY GUARD. BUT NOW YOU'LL GET TO SEE ONE, AS YOU'RE GOING TO BUILD AN ENGINE OF YOUR OWN.

TASK TWO: BUILD THE ENGINE

You need to make your car move forwards, otherwise – let's be honest – it's going to be a pretty rubbish racing car. And that means you need to make an engine.

The type of engine used in Formula 1 racing cars, and in most of the cars you see on the road, is called an "internal combustion engine". "Internal" means "inside" and "combustion" just means "burning", so "internal combustion engine" literally means "an engine that burns something inside it" – usually petrol or diesel.

But the way it really works is a bit like an ice lolly ... one of the tall, thin ones that come in a tube wrapper. When you squeeze the bottom of the lolly's wrapper it pushes the lolly up, so that you can eat the top bit – when you stop squeezing, the lolly falls back down into the wrapper again.

In an internal combustion engine, the tube wrapper is a part called a "cylinder" and the lolly, sliding within the cylinder when it's pushed, is called a "piston". The push in an engine is created by small explosions caused by burning petrol, and the movement of a strong metal pole which is attached to the piston (called a "connecting rod").

DID YOU KNOW?
THE ENGINE OF A FORMULA 1 CAR HAS SIX CYLINDERS, ARRANGED IN TWO ROWS AND FORMING A V-SHAPE. THAT'S WHY IT'S CALLED A V6 ENGINE!

22

HERE'S HOW IT ALL WORKS:

1 When the piston moves down, air and petrol are sucked into the cylinder through a tube.

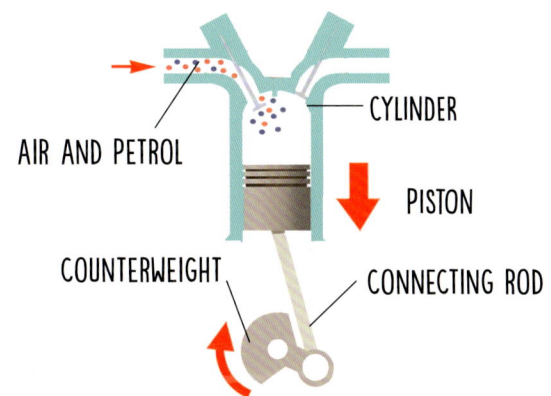

2 The connecting rod then pushes the piston up inside the cylinder. This squashes the air and petrol tightly together.

3 The petrol is set alight with a spark. The mix of petrol and air creates a small explosion, which pushes the piston down inside the cylinder again.

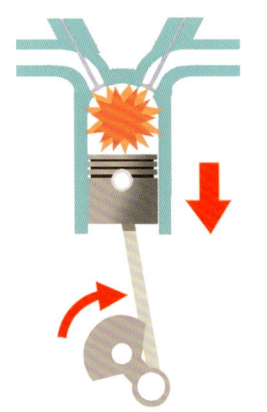

4 The counterweight keeps spinning and pushes on the connecting rod, which then pushes the piston up once more, and the fumes from the burnt petrol are pushed out through the exhaust.

5 In the six cylinders of a Formula 1 engine, the connecting rods are all attached onto the same pole, called the crankshaft. The pistons' movement makes the crankshaft rotate. The crankshaft then turns the axles that the wheels are fixed onto, and this is what makes them turn and the car go forwards.

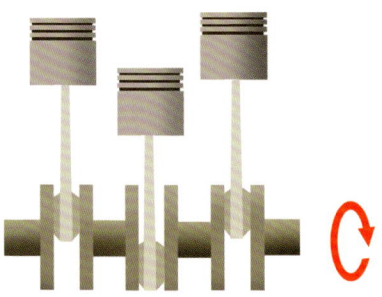

PROBLEM

There doesn't seem to be any immediate problem, so why don't we just make a mini-engine and put it in your car? Job done!

However, there IS a problem ... but it only develops over a long period of time. People have been using combustion engines like this since the 1800s, and it is now known that burning fuels like petrol and diesel is bad for the environment.

When these fuels are burnt (as they are in an engine), they release a lot of gas called carbon dioxide – and when carbon dioxide is released into the air, it makes our planet hotter. This can, over time, lead to climate change, which then causes big problems like melting sea ice, rising sea levels and more extreme weather, all of which hugely impact the natural world.

This means engineers are now looking for ways to make cars run without burning petrol or diesel, by using electricity or even solar power (energy from the sun).

SOLUTION

You are going to make an engine that doesn't need petrol, but can still make your car go at pretty impressive speeds. Believe it or not, you are going to power your racing car not with electricity, or the sun, but with (drumroll please ...) air!

DID YOU KNOW?

ALTHOUGH AIR CAN SEEM LIKE "NOTHING", IT CAN AND DOES PUSH AGAINST OBJECTS. IT DOES THIS THROUGH "AIR PRESSURE". IN A GIVEN AMOUNT OF SPACE, THE MORE AIR THERE IS, THE HIGHER THE AIR PRESSURE, AND THE HIGHER THE AIR PRESSURE, THE MORE PUSH THE AIR HAS TO MAKE SOMETHING MOVE.

HOW DOES IT WORK?

To understand how air can make things move, you only have to look at sponges. When you squash a sponge, you still have the same amount of sponge – just in a smaller space. When you release the sponge, it goes back to the size it was before.

Imagine trying to balance a pea on your sponge as it got bigger again: it would ping right off. (You might even call it an "escape-pea"…)

Strange as it may sound, given that it's not something solid you can hold in your hands, it's possible to squash air too … and, when you stop squashing it, it returns to the size it was before (like the sponge).

We're going to use this idea of squashing (which scientists call "compressing") air, and then letting it get bigger again (which scientists call "expanding"), to power your car. Your engine is going to compress air (increasing the air pressure), and then only let it expand out of a small hole at the back of the car. As the air moves backwards out of this hole, it should send your car in the opposite direction: forwards!

At least, that's the plan … and engineers love a plan. But engineers also love problem-solving, and because we know that some materials are hard to find, you have two options for building an engine.

Option 1 is a LOW-TECH way, just in case you can't find all the bits you need for Option 2. And **Option 2** is a HIGH-TECH way.

Both options will make an awesome racing car.

LET'S GET STARTED!

ASK AN ADULT TO HELP

WHAT YOU'LL NEED

BALLOON (A NORMAL-SHAPED, NORMAL-SIZED ONE IS FINE)

4-PINT PLASTIC MILK BOTTLE (EMPTY AND CLEAN)

TAPE

SCISSORS

PVC TAPE

SHARP PENCIL

STICKY TACK (A PEA-SIZED AMOUNT)

60 CM PIECE OF STRING
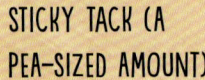

BALLOON PUMP

OPTION 1: THE LOW-TECH WAY
BALLOON ENGINE

1 Take the plastic milk bottle and ask an adult to cut off the handle. You should now have an L-shaped bit of plastic; make sure all the cut edges are smooth. (You can recycle the rest of the bottle.)

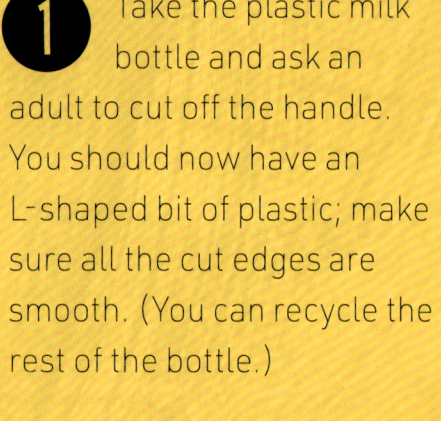

2 Put the shorter end of the handle into the opening of the balloon, so that it reaches approximately 2 cm inside the balloon.

3 Secure the balloon firmly in this position with PVC tape.

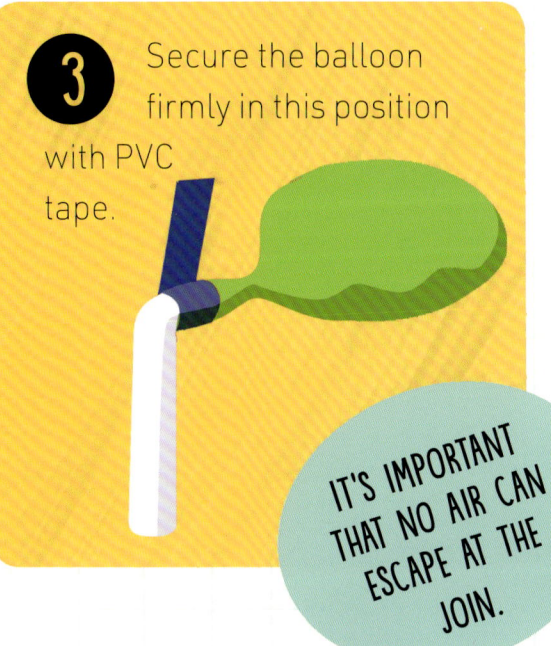

4 Inflate the balloon through the handle (using the pump) and then tightly pinch the balloon's neck, remove the pump and put your thumb in or over the end of the handle. With your thumb completely blocking the hole, release your pinch. Can you hear air escaping or see the balloon getting smaller? If so, you need to seal the area where the balloon meets the handle a bit better using more tape.

IT'S IMPORTANT THAT NO AIR CAN ESCAPE AT THE JOIN.

5 Take the pencil and at the writing end, at the place where the barrel (non-sloping part) starts, wrap PVC tape around it so that it snugly fits into the end of the handle. This should take about 30 wraps of tape.

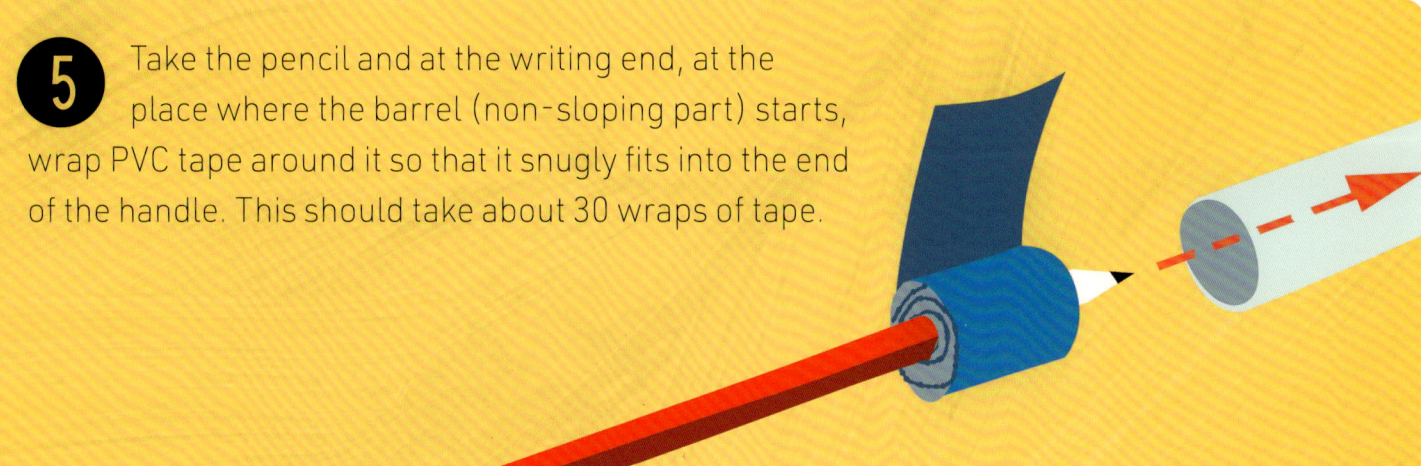

6 Mould the sticky tack around the sloping part of the pencil. We'll call this pencil-tape-sticky-tack combo your "stopper stick", and when it's in the handle you want it to stop the air escaping from the balloon.

7 You can test this by inflating the balloon and then pinching the balloon at its neck. While it's pinched, insert your stopper stick into the handle. Then, when you release your pinch on the balloon, it should stay inflated.

8 Take the string and tie one end of it onto the non-writing end of the pencil, and tape it securely to stop the knot slipping off. At the other end of the string, make a loop big enough for you to put your hand through and either tie or tape the loop into place.

28

9 It's almost time to attach your engine to the chassis you made in Chapter One, but before you do this, you need to cut a small flap in the back of the chassis. To do this, measure 2 cm in from both sides of the chassis and mark this at the back of the chassis. From each of these marks, draw a line 2 cm long up from the back of the chassis. Use scissors to cut along these two lines to make a small flap.

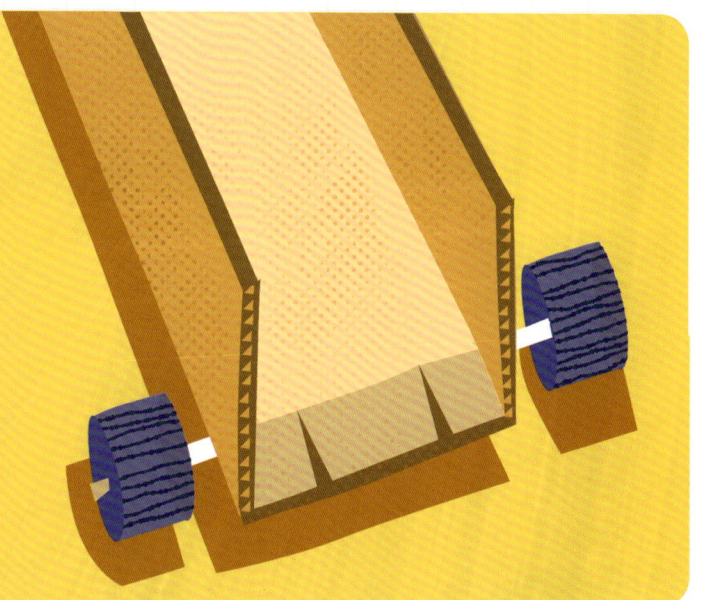

10 Lay the bottle handle flat along the base of the chassis, making sure the open end of the handle is roughly down the middle, facing the back of the chassis and hanging over the edge by approximately 2 cm. Tape the handle securely into place.

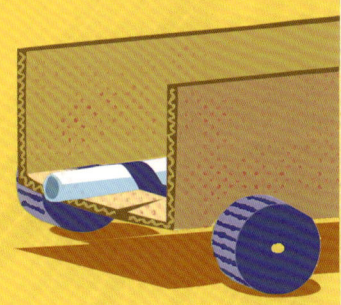

WHAT'S NEXT?

You are awesome. You've already built your car's chassis AND engine. To make your car race forward, all you'll need to do is release your stopper stick. But before we get to that, you need somewhere to race… Skip ahead and take a look at Chapter Three!

OPTION 2: THE HIGH-TECH WAY
BOTTLE ENGINE

ASK AN ADULT TO HELP

WHAT YOU'LL NEED

- 500 ML PLASTIC BOTTLE WITH LID
- INNER TUBE OF AN OLD BICYCLE TYRE
- SHARP PENCIL
- STICKY TACK (A PEA-SIZED AMOUNT)
- PEN
- SCISSORS
- A SHARP POINTY OBJECT LIKE POINTY SCISSORS, CORKSCREW OR KEYS
- PVC TAPE
- GLUE
- BICYCLE PUMP
- 60 CM PIECE OF STRING
- LIGHTER AND HEATPROOF GLOVE (OPTIONAL)

REMEMBER ALL THE SAFETY ADVICE!

1 Remove the lid from the bottle. Using the scissors (and with an adult's help), make a hole in the lid that is just big enough to fit the "valve" of the inner tube – the valve being the sticky-out metal part.

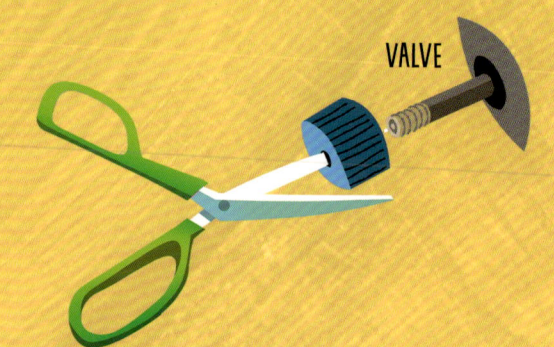

VALVE

2 Push the valve through the hole, making sure the valve sits on the outside of the lid, and draw around the bottom of the lid onto the tube.

3 Cut around the line you've just drawn and then squash this rubber circle into the very top of the lid, from the inside up. The valve should poke through the hole.

TOP TIP

ENSURE THE RUBBER IS SQUASHED ALL THE WAY INTO THE VERY TOP OF THE LID, OTHERWISE THE LID WON'T SEAL PROPERLY.

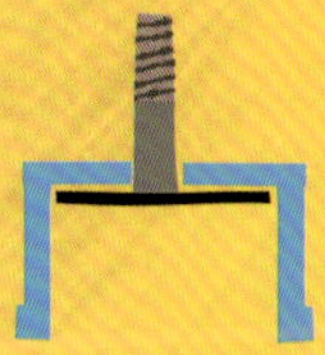

4 Screw the lid onto the bottle, then use the bicycle pump to add air through the valve. Try about 2–5 pumps, but be careful not to put too much air in, in case of any loose parts. You don't need much: this is just an air test. Do you hear any air escaping? If so, try to find where the leaks are and seal them with tape or glue. Once the bottle is airtight, remove the lid so it's not under pressure for the next bit.

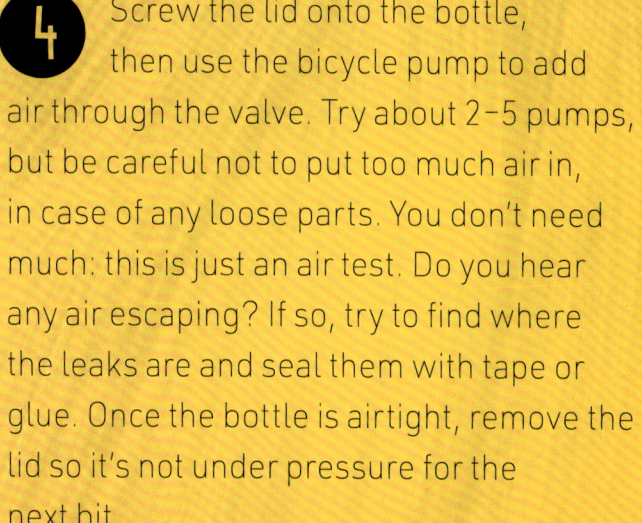

TOP TIP

FOR AN EASIER WAY TO MAKE THE HOLE, ASK AN ADULT TO HEAT UP THE METAL POINTY OBJECT FOR 30 SECONDS USING THE LIGHTER (WHILE WEARING A HEATPROOF GLOVE) SO THAT IT PIERCES THROUGH THE PLASTIC OF THE BOTTLE MORE EASILY.

5 With an adult's help, use the pointy object (scissors, key, corkscrew, etc.) to make a tiny hole in the base of the bottle. This hole can be anywhere in the base (the thinner the plastic, the easier the hole will be to make), but it needs to be small enough for the tip of the pencil (the sloping part) to block it. Making the hole IS difficult: be careful not to let your sharp object slip on the bottle. It WILL take a while to get through the base, but keep going. I believe in you.

6 Push the pencil into the newly formed hole. The tip (sloping part) of the pencil should block the hole.

7 Remove the pencil and, at the place where the barrel (non-sloping part) of the pencil starts, wrap PVC tape tightly around it. Wrap this tape round twenty times, so your pencil starts to look like one of those mini sausage rolls (mmm, yummy).

8 Now, take the sticky tack and mould it around the sloping part of the pencil. This pencil-tape-sticky-tack combo is your "stopper stick", and should now fit very snugly into the hole in the bottle.

TOP TIP

IF YOUR PENCIL IS STILL TOO SMALL, USE MORE TAPE OR STICKY TACK UNTIL IT'S A TIGHT FIT. IF THE PENCIL IS TOO BIG, MAKE THE HOLE A TEENY BIT BIGGER UNTIL IT FITS SNUGLY.

TOP TIP

IF YOU DRAW A MARK ON THE PENCIL, YOU'LL BE ABLE TO COUNT EACH TIME YOU PASS IT WITH THE TAPE. THIS WILL HELP YOU KEEP TRACK OF HOW MANY TIMES YOU'VE WRAPPED IT AROUND THE PENCIL.

18, 19, 20 ... AND THAT'S A WRAP!

9 Take the string and tie one end of it onto the non-pointy end of the pencil, and use tape to stop the knot from sliding off. Then make a loop (big enough for you to put your hand through) at the other end of the string, which you can either tie or secure with tape.

TOP TIP
TWISTING AND PUSHING THE STOPPER STICK AT THE SAME TIME WORKS BEST TO GET IT TO PROPERLY BLOCK THE HOLE IN THE BOTTLE.

WHAT'S NEXT?
You are awesome. You've already built your car's chassis AND engine. To make your car race forward, all you'll need to do is release your stopper stick. But before you can do that you need somewhere to race...

10 Now you need to attach your engine to your chassis. To do this, lay the bottle flat on the cardboard chassis you made in Chapter One, making sure that the valve is facing the front and the hole is right at the back of the chassis. Rotate the bottle so the hole is close to the base of the chassis. Next, simply tape the bottle securely into place.

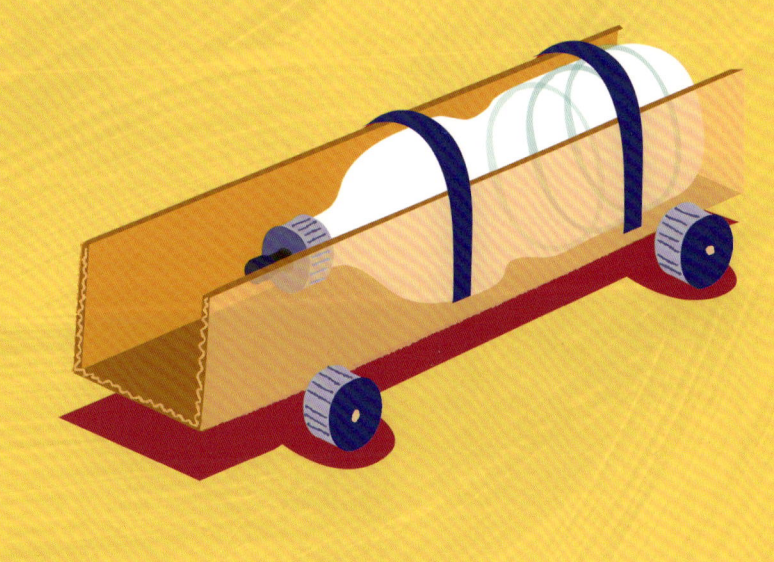

THE START GATE

CHAPTER THREE

TO REALLY BECOME THE WORLD-CLASS RACING CAR DRIVER WE BOTH KNOW YOU'RE GOING TO BE, YOU ACTUALLY NEED TO TAKE PART IN RACES. AND A RACE NEEDS (AMONG LOTS OF OTHER THINGS) AN ULTRA-DRAMATIC START. OK, SO THE DRAMA MAY NOT BE NEEDED, BUT THE START GATE REALLY IS (AS YOU'RE ABOUT TO FIND OUT).

PROBLEM

Imagine trying to juggle custard at the same time as doing a handstand. Each thing is tricky enough on its own, let alone trying to do them both at the same time!

Sometimes it can feel a bit like that when you're trying to solve engineering problems – as though you've got too many things to try to do at once. At this point in the book we've got to tackle one of those tricky situations, because, the way things currently are, to make your car "go" you'd have to hold on to the chassis, pull out the stopper stick AND release the car at exactly the right time ... all on your own.

What you need is something to help you launch your car more easily: something strong enough to support your racing car, so that you can pull out the stopper stick without having to hold on to your car. And it would also be handy if this "something" marked the beginning of your race, wouldn't it?

SOLUTION

You're going to make yourself a START GATE, with long sides so that, even when it's pushed against, it shouldn't tip over.

ASK AN ADULT TO HELP

WHAT YOU'LL NEED

RULER – THE LONGER, THE BETTER

PEN OR PENCIL

50 CM BY 10 CM PIECE OF REALLY STIFF CARDBOARD

10 CM BY 40 CM PIECES OF STIFF CARDBOARD (X2)

54 CM BY 9 CM PIECE OF STIFF CARDBOARD

WOODEN KEBAB SKEWERS (AT LEAST 20 CM LONG) (X2)

TAPE/ALL-PURPOSE GLUE

SCISSORS

THE START GATE

1 Take the 50 cm by 10 cm piece of cardboard and draw a line that is halfway between the two long edges (so, 5 cm away from each). Make sure the line goes all the way along the cardboard.

2 Make a mark at 11 cm, 13 cm, 24 cm, 26 cm, 37 cm and 39 cm along the line.

3 Just in from one of the long edges, make more marks at the same points as in step 2: so, at 11 cm, 13 cm, 24 cm, 26 cm, 37 cm and 39 cm.

4 Draw a line between the two marks made at 11 cm. Draw a second line between the two marks made at 13 cm. Repeat all the way along the long line. You should now have a line with three narrow rectangles sticking out from it.

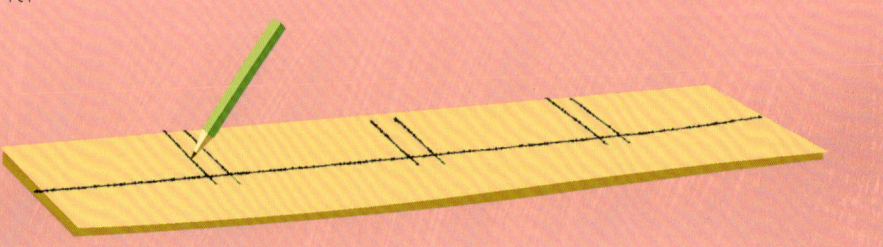

THE STOPPER STICK SHOULD POKE OUT THROUGH THE HOLE IN THE CARDBOARD. IF IT DOESN'T, YOU'LL NEED TO CUT THE RECTANGLES SO THAT THEY'RE A LITTLE BIT LONGER.

5 Using your scissors, cut out these three narrow rectangles. You have now made the "backstop" for the start gate: the back of your car will be pushed up against this section when the race starts. To test if it works, put the stopper stick into your car and rest the back of your car against the piece of cardboard – with the three holes you just cut out facing downwards. Poke the stopper stick through one of the three holes.

6 Take the two pieces of cardboard that measure 10 cm by 40 cm and draw a line 5 cm in from one of their short edges. Fold both pieces of cardboard at these lines to make flaps, which you will use to attach these "side pieces" onto the "backstop". Attach the side pieces onto the backstop using glue or tape, to make a U-shaped piece of cardboard (with the backstop between the two side pieces).

7 Measure 5 cm in from the end of one of the side pieces (at the free end, not the end attached to the backstop) and make a mark. Repeat with the other side piece.

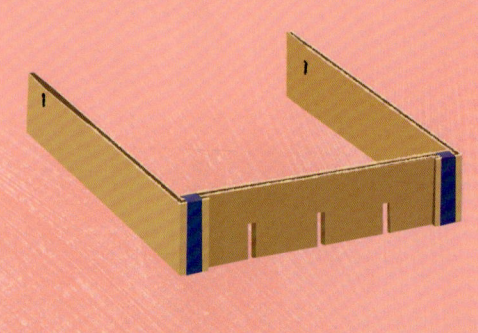

8 Using glue or tape, attach one kebab stick onto the cardboard at each of these marks, so that they are sticking up into the air.

TOP TIP
IF YOU'VE MADE THE BALLOON ENGINE, YOU MAY NEED TO STICK TWO KEBAB STICKS TOGETHER TO MAKE THE GATE TALL ENOUGH.

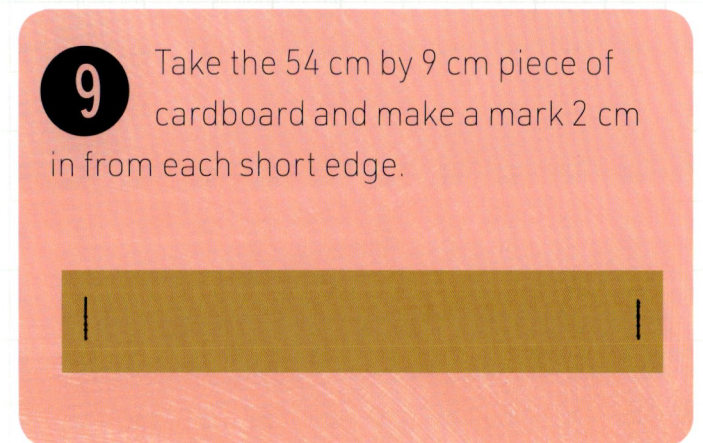

9 Take the 54 cm by 9 cm piece of cardboard and make a mark 2 cm in from each short edge.

10 Glue or tape the free ends of the kebab sticks from the side pieces onto this piece of cardboard, at the marks you've just drawn.

11 You now have your start gate. There'll be a backstop, sides, and a large "gantry" across the top.

IF YOU CAN'T FIND STIFF CARD, GLUE TWO PIECES TOGETHER.

WHAT'S NEXT?

Time for you and your car to make your racing debut! ("Debut" is a great word, isn't it? It's pronounced "day-bew" and is a French word that means "a first".) So, are you ready to make your first ever outing as a racing car driver? I said, ARE YOU READY? You'd better be, because that's exactly what you're going to do next...

CHAPTER FOUR

READY TO RACE

IT. IS. ON!

AND BY "IT", I OBVIOUSLY MEAN TWO THINGS: THE FIRST BEING YOUR FAVOURITE RACING OVERALLS, AND THE SECOND BEING A CRASH HELMET SO HEAVY THAT IT FEELS LIKE YOU'RE WEARING A WATERMELON!

With your racing gear on and your car now built,
you are as ready as you'll ever be. Time to step out of the
workshop: your time as a racing driver has finally come.
You lower yourself into the cockpit of your car, move into position
at the start line and give your teammates a knowing nod. The only thing
you can hear is the sound of revving engines.

A red light appears on the gantry ... then another ... then one more.
Eventually all five are lit up. You're waiting: waiting for all of those lights to
go out. Because when they do that's your signal that the race has begun.

BOOM: THE LIGHTS ARE OUT AND YOU ARE OFF!

OK, that was a nice bit of (imaginary) practice.
Here's how you get going for real...

ASK AN ADULT TO HELP

THE RACE

WHAT YOU'LL NEED

YOUR CAR

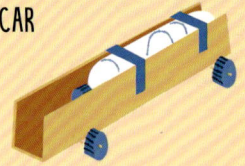

YOUR START GATE

IF YOU MADE THE LOW-TECH ENGINE: BALLOON PUMP

IF YOU MADE THE HIGH-TECH ENGINE: BICYCLE PUMP WITH A PRESSURE GAUGE (A PRESSURE GAUGE IS A DIAL WITH NUMBERS ON, WHICH WILL SHOW YOU HOW MUCH PRESSURE THE AIR HAS)

A SMOOTH SURFACE TO RACE ON, LIKE A WOODEN OR TILED FLOOR (NOT A RUG OR CARPET)

SUNGLASSES OR SAFETY GOGGLES

1 Put your sunglasses or safety goggles on and lay the start gate on a smooth floor.

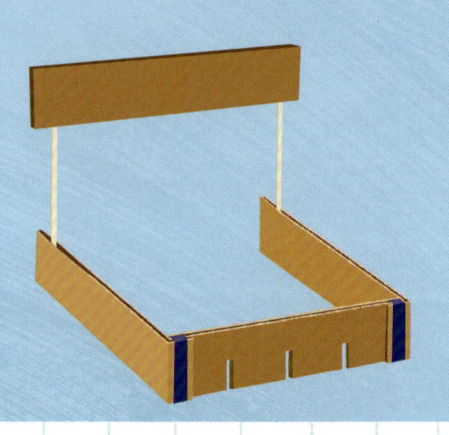

2 If you're using a bottle engine, insert the stopper stick firmly into the bottle, making sure it properly blocks the hole. If you're using a balloon engine, skip this step.

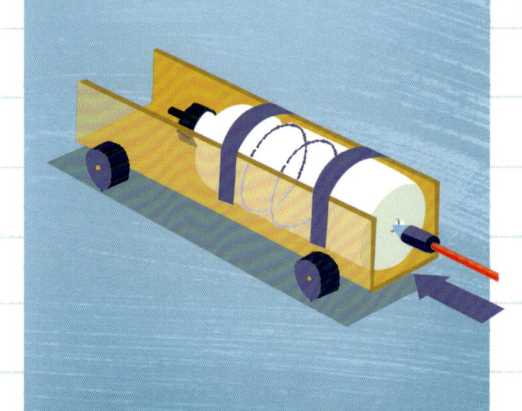

3 Place the loop of string around your wrist. This is important – see safety tip below.

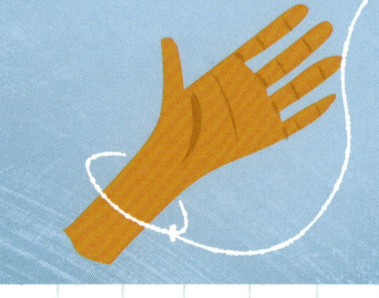

SAFETY TIP

ONCE IT'S IN THE BOTTLE, HOLD THE STOPPER STICK FIRMLY IN PLACE AND NEVER POINT IT TOWARDS YOUR EYE OR ANYONE ELSE'S. THE SAFETY STRING AROUND YOUR WRIST IS THERE TO STOP THE STICK GOING TOO FAR IF ANYTHING GOES WRONG.

4 **A.** If you're using a bottle engine, connect the bike pump to the valve of the inner tube (remember, that's the metal bit that sticks out) and use the pump to increase the pressure and compress the air inside the bottle. See step 5 for how much you'll need to pump!

B. If you're using a balloon engine, pump the balloon up through the plastic handle using the balloon pump.

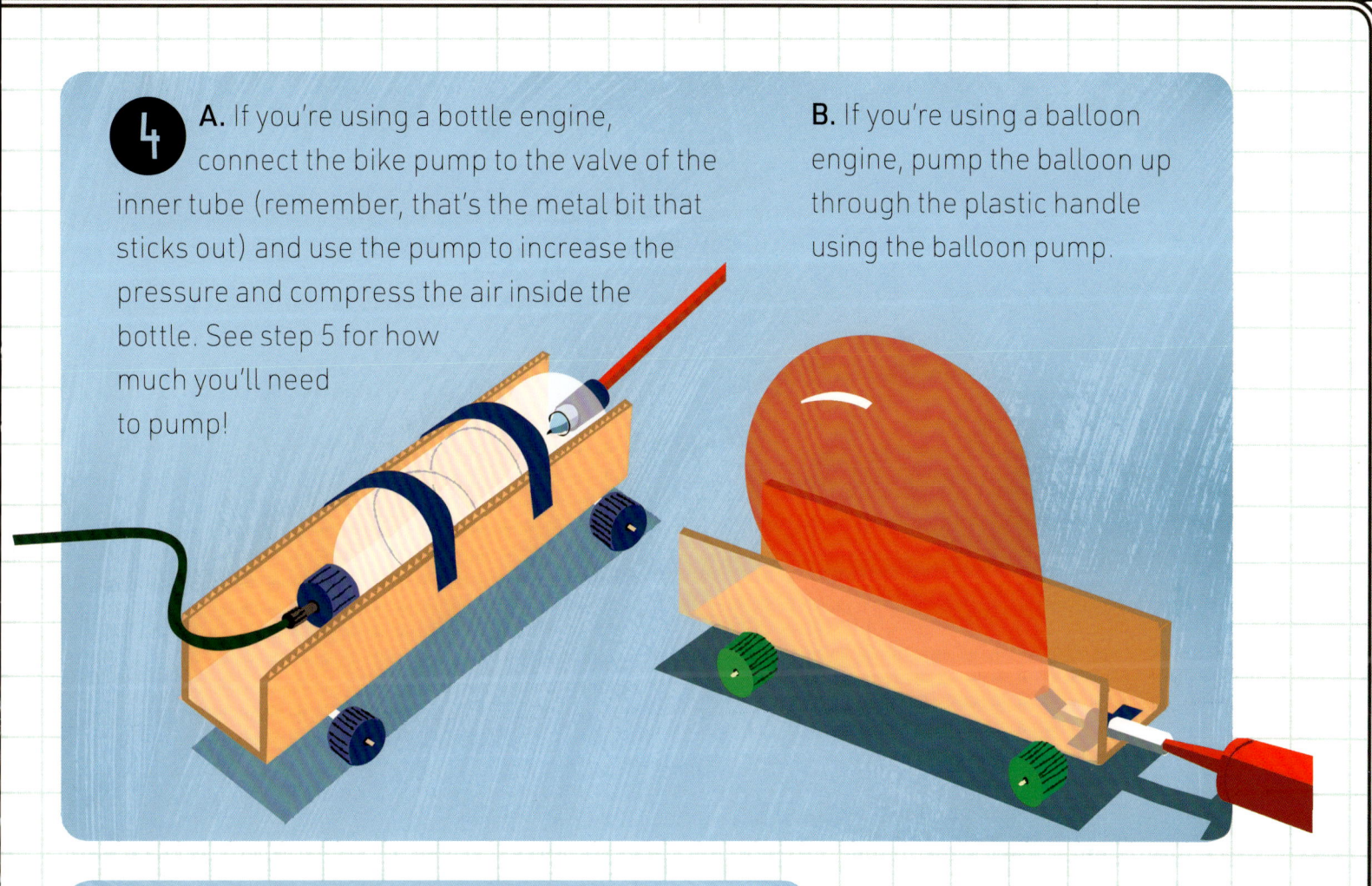

5 Keep on pumping until the balloon is fully inflated, or until the pressure in the bottle has reached approximately 30–40 psi (approximately 2–3 bar). Never go beyond 50 psi!

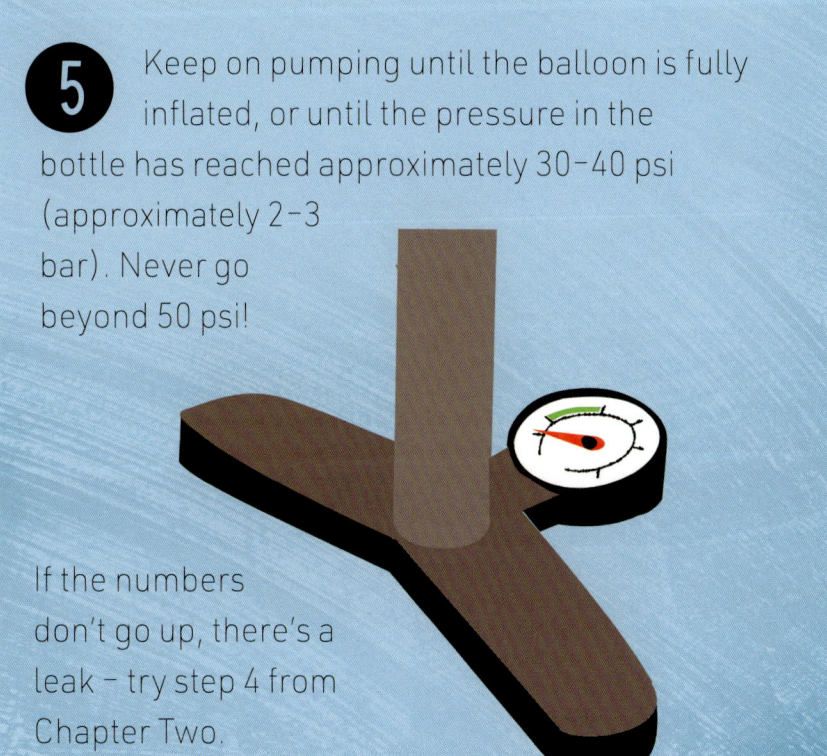

If the numbers don't go up, there's a leak – try step 4 from Chapter Two.

SAFETY TIP
YOU NEED TWO PEOPLE FOR THE BOTTLE ENGINE: ONE TO HOLD THE STICK AND THE OTHER TO USE THE PUMP.

6 If you're using the balloon engine, insert your stopper stick. To do this, pinch the fully inflated balloon at its opening and keep pinching as you insert the stopper stick into the handle. Once it's in place, you can release your pinch on the balloon and it should stay inflated.

7 If you're using the bottle engine, carefully remove the pump. The air should stay inside the bottle.

8 Place your car just in front of the backstop of the start gate: the stopper stick can poke through any of the three rectangles.

9 With the back of the car against the backstop, firmly hold on to both the stopper stick and the backstop. Now firmly tug on the stopper stick.

REMINDER: NEVER POINT THE STOPPER STICK TOWARDS ANYONE'S EYE.

TOP TIP
THE MIDDLE RECTANGLE IS BEST TO USE WHEN RACING ONE CAR, WHEREAS THE TWO SIDE RECTANGLES ARE BEST IF YOU HAVE TWO CARS TO RACE.

10 As the stopper stick is pulled out, your car should whizz forwards!

DID YOU KNOW?
RACING CARS TEND TO WORK BEST WHEN THEIR TYRES AND ENGINES ARE WARMED UP, SO IN A RACE THERE IS USUALLY ONE LAP WHICH IS A WARM-UP LAP BEFORE THE CARS START RACING PROPERLY. THIS IS CALLED A "FORMATION LAP".

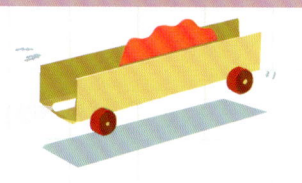

WHAT'S NEXT?
This is where things get really interesting. Did your car work as planned? If it didn't, then you might actually be one of the lucky ones! You get to experience what being a proper engineer is all about: testing and tweaking to improve a design.

And if your car did work, then HOORAY! That's awesome! But do you know what's even more awesome? Making your car run even better than it did first time around.

LET'S GO F.A.R.T.!

MAYBE WE NEED A NEW NAME...

CHAPTER FIVE

TESTING & TWEAKING

THIS IS WHERE THE REAL FUN BEGINS... Time to really make this car your own. When something isn't quite the way you wanted it to be the first time, it can be frustrating – but when you finally solve that problem, it's the best feeling ever. And this is what being an engineer is all about.

When the inventor Thomas Edison and his team were trying to perfect the light bulb, they didn't get it right first time. When things weren't quite going according to plan, it's reported Edison said, "I have not failed. I've just found 10,000 ways that won't work."

And, to be honest, he's totally right. Building new things isn't easy. But we need to be brave enough to have a go and know that on the road to getting things right, there will be times when things go wrong.

> 9,998, 9,999, 10,000...

> HE'S ABOUT TO HAVE HIS LIGHT BULB MOMENT!

So, run your car once, twice, twenty times. What do you notice? Maybe an adult can help you take a video of your car in motion (perhaps even in slow motion), so that you can rewatch it carefully.

Does it spin around in a circle, rather than drive in a straight line?

Does it bounce upwards, instead of keeping in contact with the floor?

If so, have a look through the following make-my-car-better tips, which will show you how to fix some problems you may have and how to generally ... well ... make your car better!

ASK AN ADULT TO HELP

TIP 1 ADD A REAR WING

WE'RE NOT TALKING ABOUT A BIG FEATHERED NUMBER ON THE BACK OF YOUR CAR (THOUGH IF THAT'S YOUR THING, GO FOR IT). THIS IS ABOUT BUILDING ONE OF THOSE TRAYS THAT STICK UP AT THE BACK OF SOME RACING CARS.

PROBLEM
Believe it or not, even cars weighing 800 kg can lift up from the road. This is bad from a big-lump-of-metal-flying-uncontrollably-through-the-air point of view, but it's also rubbish in terms of racing. To go fast and to get the most grip, a Formula 1 car's tyres need to be in contact with the road as much as possible – so the car needs lots of downforce. (Refresh your training on pages 10–11 if you need a reminder about downforce!)

SOLUTION
To increase the amount of downforce and the contact the tyres have with the road, engineers add parts onto the car that change how the air is affected as the car drives through it. These are called wings, and you can have "front" and "rear" wings.

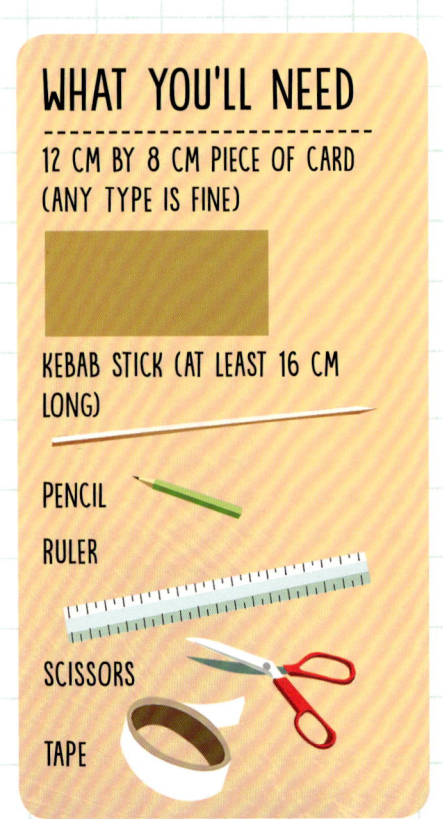

WHAT YOU'LL NEED

12 CM BY 8 CM PIECE OF CARD (ANY TYPE IS FINE)

KEBAB STICK (AT LEAST 16 CM LONG)

PENCIL

RULER

SCISSORS

TAPE

HERE'S HOW TO MAKE A REAR WING:

1 Measure a line 1.5 cm in from the long edge of the piece of card. Mark it with a pencil and then fold along the line so that the card is slightly bent.

48

2 Get an adult to help cut the kebab stick into two 8 cm pieces.

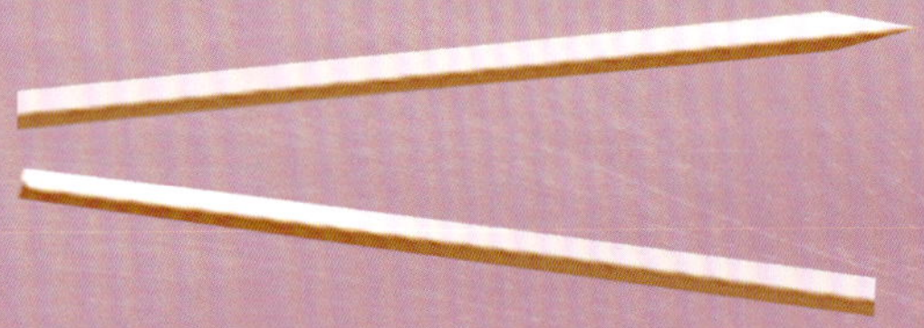

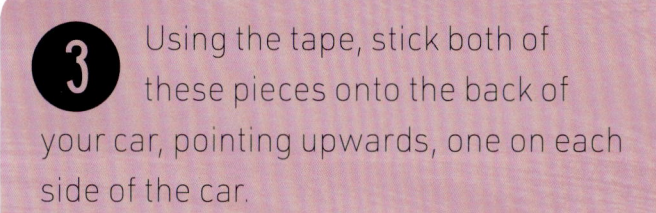

GET AN ADULT TO HELP!

3 Using the tape, stick both of these pieces onto the back of your car, pointing upwards, one on each side of the car.

4 On the folded-over bit of the card (the 1.5 cm wide bit), make a mark 2 cm in from the short edge at both ends.

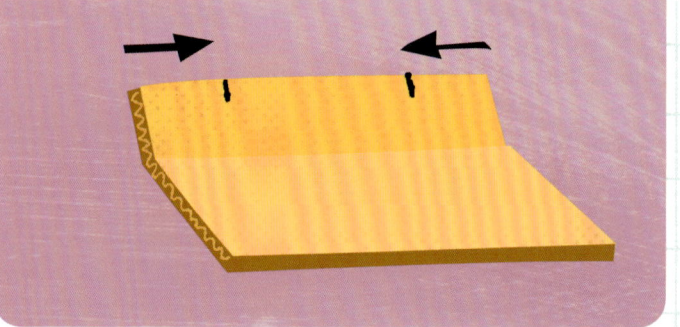

5 Line these marks up with the kebab sticks and tape into place.

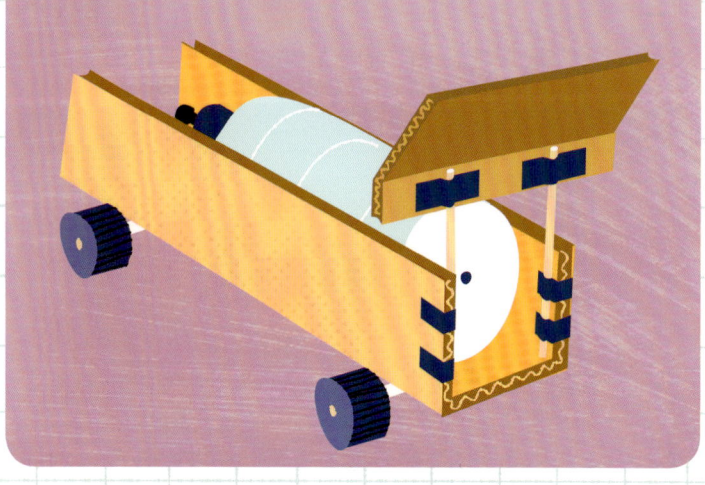

TOP TIP
FOR EXTRA STABILITY, TAPE THE KEBAB STICKS ONTO THE INSIDE OF YOUR RACING CAR AND MAKE SURE THEY'RE TOUCHING THE BASE OF THE CHASSIS.

ASK AN ADULT TO HELP

TIP 2 ADD A FRONT WING

ALWAYS AT THE BACK OF THE PACK? IF YOUR CAR IS TOO SLOW, THIS MAY BE WHAT YOU NEED.

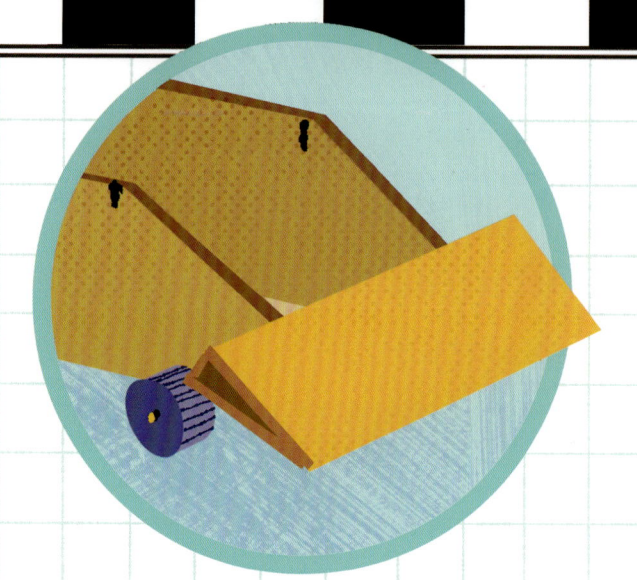

PROBLEM

The speed of a car depends on a whole heap of factors. One of these is how much air the car has to push against when it drives forwards. At the moment your car is a bit ... well ... boxy. This means it pushes against a lot of air, which can slow your car down. What a drag!

SOLUTION

To make cars zoom along in the most efficient way, engineers think carefully about their shape. If the front of the car is pointy, it can cut through the air and push it out of the car's path – this reduces the drag on the car, making it more aerodynamic and allowing it to go faster. So when engineers are designing the front wings of the car, they make sure that they are pointy!

WHAT YOU'LL NEED

12 CM BY 8 CM PIECE OF CARD (ANY TYPE IS FINE)

SHARP PENCIL

RULER

ALL-PURPOSE GLUE

TAPE

SCISSORS

HERE'S HOW TO MAKE A POINTED FRONT WING:

1 From one of the long edges of the card measure 3 cm and then 4.5 cm down.

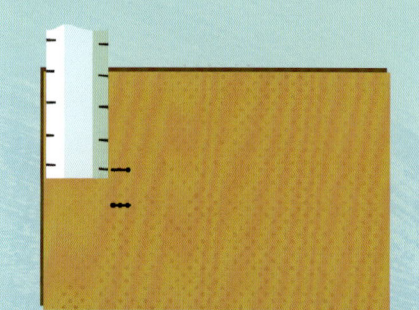

2 At both of these points, make a line all the way across the card. Using the sharp pencil and ruler, score both lines.

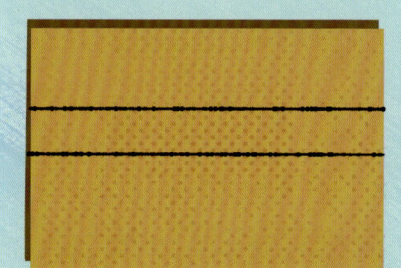

50

3 Fold along both lines so that the card is bent back on itself and the two long edges are level with each other.

4 Glue into place. (You may need to use tape to hold the card in position as the glue dries.)

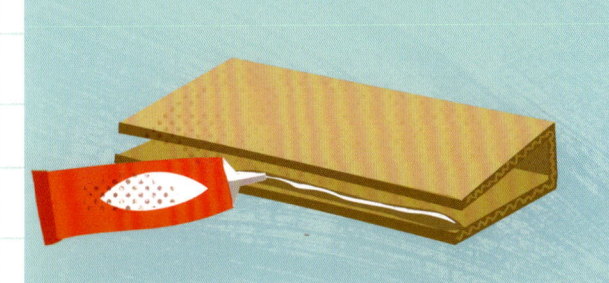

5 Meanwhile, measure 9 cm along both sides of your car from the front, and make a mark at these points.

6 Draw a diagonal line from these points down to where each side of the car meets the front base.

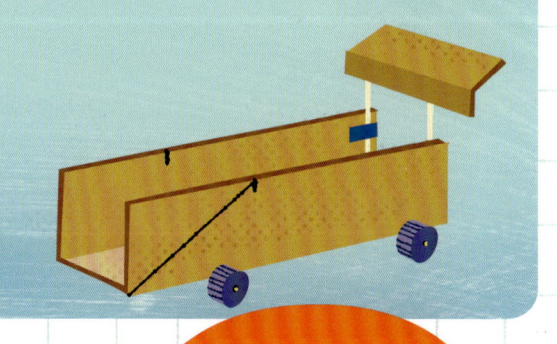

7 Cut along these lines, to create a sloping front. Once the separate piece of card is dry, tape or glue this into position on the front of your car at the bottom of this slope (with the longer side facing up).

TOP TIP
REMOVING YOUR CAR'S ENGINE (BOTTLE OR BALLOON) WILL MAKE THESE STEPS EASIER.

51

ASK AN ADULT TO HELP

TIP 3 ADD TYRES

YOU'VE ALREADY GOT WHEELS, BUT ADDING TYRES SHOULD IMPROVE THEIR GRIP AND HELP THEM TO SPIN BETTER.

WHAT YOU'LL NEED

BICYCLE INNER TUBE (THE SAME ONE YOU USED BEFORE, IF YOU MADE THE HIGH-TECH ENGINE)

PENCIL

RULER

SCISSORS

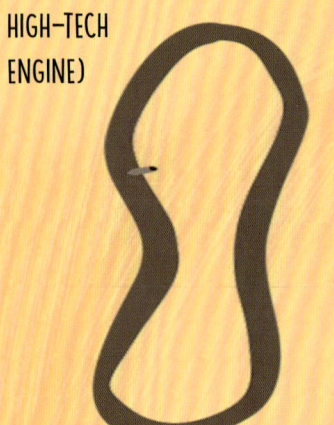

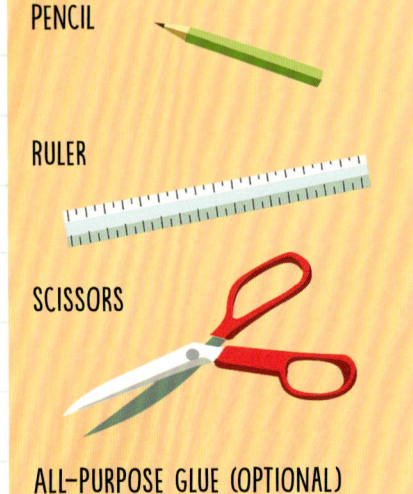

ALL-PURPOSE GLUE (OPTIONAL)

PROBLEM

The wheels on your car aren't turning properly. Now, this is a downer on your car, but on a Formula 1 car it would be a total nightmare. This is because your car gets its push from the air coming out of the bottle or balloon, whereas a Formula 1 car is ONLY pushed forward by the engine turning its wheels. So, if the wheels aren't turning, the car will go nowhere. Not great for a race!

SOLUTION

The answer to this is pretty simple: add tyres! Tyres are the rubber rings around wheels which help them grip on to the road (or kitchen floor). Wheels need that little bit of grip, so that they can turn properly.

1 Lay the inner tube out in a circle shape. Squash it flat at one point, and use scissors to cut all the way through the inner tube. Instead of having a circle of rubber tube, you should now have a straight bit of rubber.

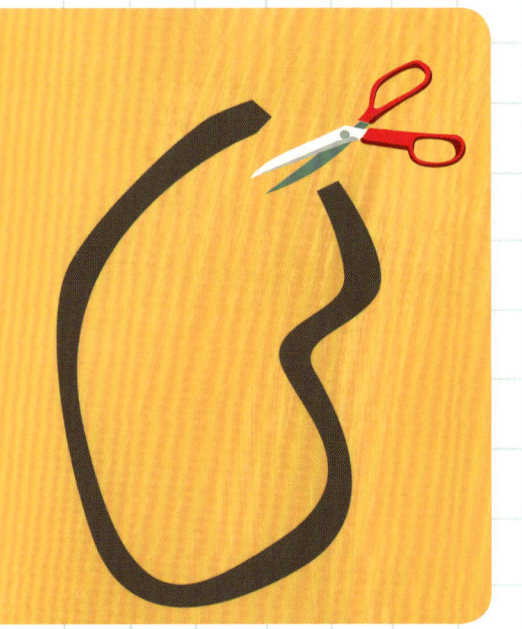

2 Measure 1 cm from the end of the tube and cut here, so you get a circle of rubber 1 cm wide.

3 Repeat step 2 three more times.

4 You'll now have four rings of rubber, each 1 cm wide. These are your tyres.

5 Carefully stretch your tyres around your bottle-top wheels – they should fit snugly. If they don't, you can always cut the rubber to size and glue it into place.

TOP TIP
IF YOUR WHEELS STILL DON'T SPIN, CHECK THAT THE KEBAB STICKS THE WHEELS ARE ATTACHED TO ARE SPINNING FREELY IN THE PAPER TUBES AND HAVEN'T GOT STUCK TO THEM BY ACCIDENT.

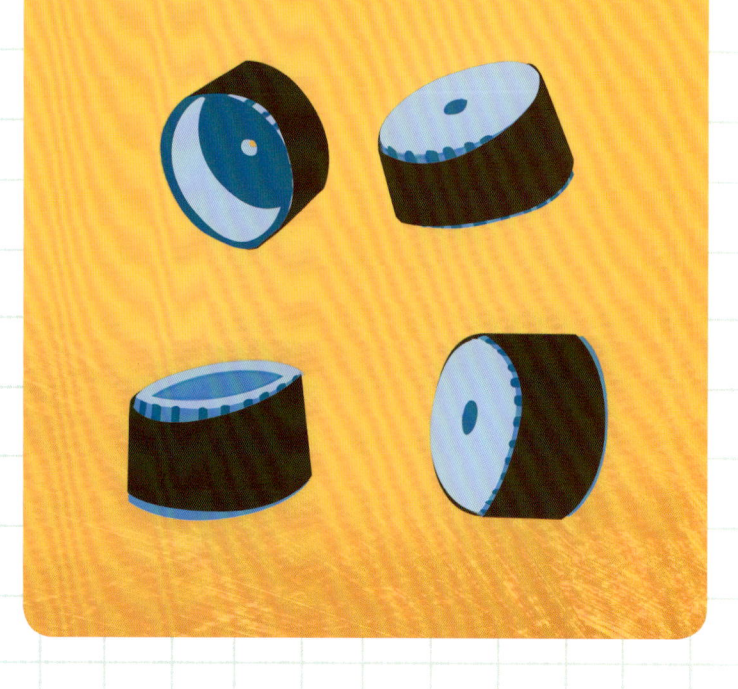

ASK AN ADULT TO HELP

TIP 4 DRIVE STRAIGHT(ER)

YOUR CAR GOES FAST ... AWESOME. YOUR CAR GOES FAST IN A CIRCLE ... NOT SO AWESOME.

PROBLEM
Your car may be speedy, but if it moves in a circle rather than going in a straight line then it isn't going to get anywhere particularly fast.

SOLUTION
There are a few reasons why your car may not be driving in a straight line. Try these different tweaks and hopefully one should work for you.

SPINNING: TROUBLESHOOTING

1. Check that the axles are straight, and also that the wheels are straight on the axles. If not, tweak them so they are. (You can glue them into place if you need.)

2. Are your wheels strong enough? Remember that tops from fizzy drink bottles work best.

If neither of these has fixed the problem then the "wheel" cause of the spinning is probably the way the air is being pushed out of the hole.

IF YOU HAVE A BALLOON ENGINE:

Ensure the handle is pointing directly backwards and not to one side.

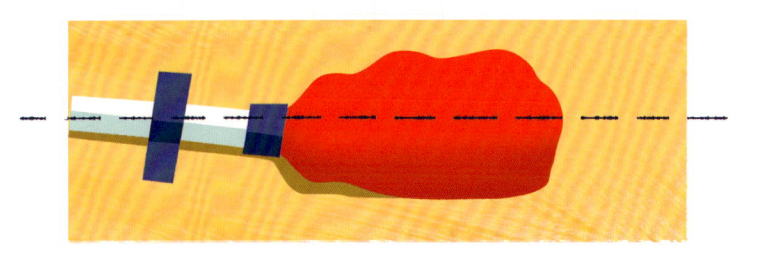

IF YOU HAVE A BOTTLE ENGINE:

1. Make sure that the hole in your bottle is pointing straight backwards and not to one side.

2. Add some weight ... but in the right place. Yes, overall your car needs to be light, but adding weight is not always bad. Here, adding weight to the front of your car will help to push the front wheels into the floor, keeping the car driving straight. A large marble-sized blob of sticky tack stuck just by the front wing should do the trick.

DID YOU KNOW?

THE CHOICE OF TYRES FOR A FORMULA 1 CAR CAN WIN OR LOSE YOU THE RACE. REALLY SMOOTH TYRES (CALLED "SLICKS") HELP THE CAR GO FAST, BUT CAUSE SLIDING IN THE RAIN. OTHER TYRES HAVE MORE GROOVES IN THEM, SO ARE BETTER IN WET CONDITIONS BUT SLOWER IN THE DRY. EACH CAR IS ALLOWED TO USE 28 TYRES PER RACE. THESE CAN BE CHANGED DURING PIT STOPS.

WHAT'S NEXT?

Your car is working perfectly, but does it LOOK like a racing car? Being an engineer isn't just about making things work well, it's also about making them look great. Where are the team colours? The logo?

IT'S TIME TO PERSONALIZE YOUR CAR...

CHAPTER SIX
PERSONALIZATION

LET PEOPLE KNOW YOUR CAR BELONGS TO YOU BY PERSONALIZING IT. YOU CAN DO THIS BY ADDING COLOURS, NUMBERS, DESIGNS OR ANYTHING ELSE YOU CAN THINK OF.

MY NEW LOOK IS ON FIRE!

SOOO FLAME-BOYANT!

What you do is completely up to you, but there are a few templates here which might help. You could give your car a number, so everyone can see which one is yours when it's rocketing away from the start gate, or you could add logos to your front and rear wings, or design posters for the side of the start gate … whatever you want! I decorated my own car so that it looked exactly the way I wanted it to: I also painted it, to make it look super slick.

What are you waiting for? Get thinking, drawing, colouring in… Make this car as awesome as you are.

DID YOU KNOW?
FORMULA 1 DRIVERS CAN CHOOSE ANY NUMBER BELOW 100 TO USE ON THE CAR THEY DRIVE, BUT THERE ARE TWO EXCEPTIONS: 1 AND 17. THE NUMBER 1 CAN ONLY BE USED BY THE CURRENT WORLD CHAMPION (THOUGH THEY DON'T HAVE TO USE IT). NUMBER 17 USED TO BE THE NUMBER OF A FRENCH DRIVER CALLED JULES BIANCHI — BUT AFTER HE DIED IN 2015, OTHER DRIVERS STOPPED USING IT, AS A SIGN OF RESPECT.

TEMPLATES

TO USE THESE TEMPLATES, SIMPLY TRACE AROUND THEM ONTO PAPER, COLOUR THEM IN, CUT THEM OUT AND STICK THEM ONTO YOUR CAR OR START GATE. TA-DAH!

NUMBER TEMPLATES FOR THE SIDE OF YOUR CAR

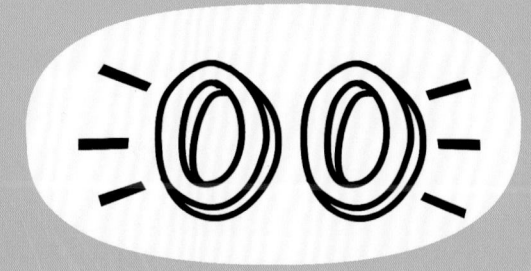

FRONT WING TEMPLATES

REAR WING TEMPLATE

REAR WING TEMPLATE

START GATE GANTRY TEMPLATE

START

START GATE ADVERTISING BOARD TEMPLATES

TASTY

RECYCLE!

SPEEDY TYRES

YUM!

READY, SET ... GO!

AND THERE YOU HAVE IT – YOUR VERY OWN RACING CAR! SO, HOW DO YOU RACE AGAINST OTHER PEOPLE?

It's simple! Just follow these final few steps:

1. Buy this book for all your friends for their birthdays. (Or just lending them your copy works too.)

2. Wait (patiently) for them to make their cars.

3. Set your start gate up on a smooth floor and make a (removable) mark 3 or 4 metres in front of the gate (this is your finish line).

4. Two at a time, pump your cars up and then place them into the start gate, just in front of the backstop. Use the two side holes in the backstop and keep the middle one free.

5. Release the cars!

6. Enjoy yourself!

And speaking of enjoying yourself, it has been an utter pleasure to help you on the road to building your very own racing car. I hope you're now holding your car and grinning from ear to ear. If so, don't stop there – making is about building things, but it's also about making something you might not expect: mistakes. Mistakes are all part of it. So now you've built your car, what else could you make? Even if you may not get it right first time!

GOODBYE FOR NOW, FRAN

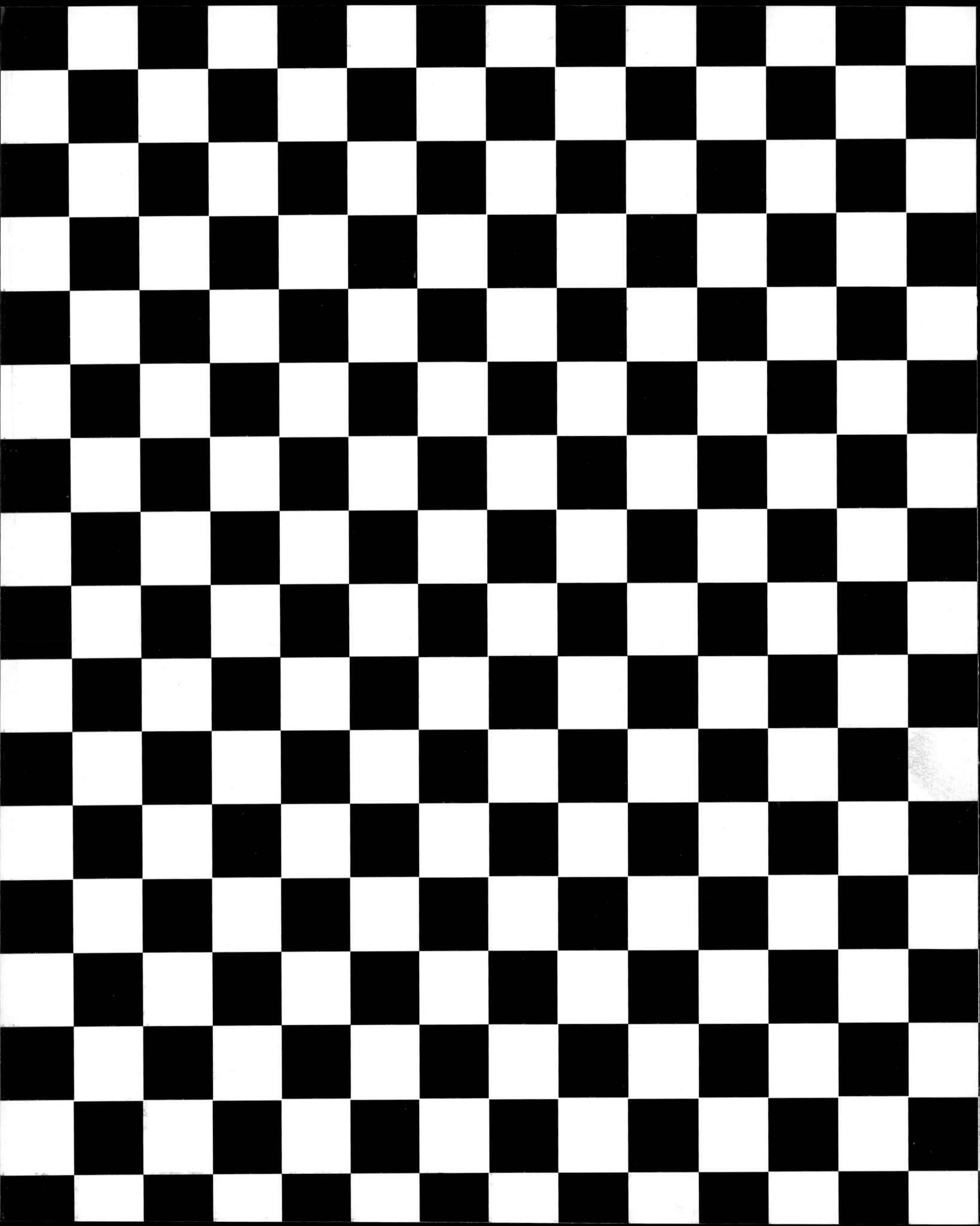